Whimsy
the Talking Pony

Whimsy
the Talking Pony

by Sandy Duval

Willowisp
Press

Text illustrations by Sandy Duval

Cover illustration by Jim Kersell

For Seth, Justin . . .
and their own Whimsy.

1

Jamie and his dad walked down the aisle of the auction barn. The air inside the dimly lit building was hot. Every pen was filled with restless animals. They were milling around and switching their tails at flies.

Jamie's father was looking over the baby lambs and calves. Today Jamie wasn't interested in lambs or calves. His dad had promised him a pony for his birthday. Today was the day.

"Come on, Dad," said Jamie, pulling Mr. Hill by the hand. "We've got to look those ponies over before the sale starts."

"We've got plenty of time," his dad told him. "They'll be selling the sheep, pigs and cows before they even get to the horses."

"But all the seats will be taken if we don't hurry!" Jamie hurried off. "I'm going to look," he called back over his shoulder.

He ran past rows of pens until he got to the pony section. There he slowed down. He looked carefully at each animal in every stall. He saw fat sleek ponies. Their owners were putting a last minute polish on their coats or talking to people who might want to buy. These ponies stood by ones and twos in pens filled with fresh hay.

There were other pens jammed full of dusty, sweating ponies. As they kicked the flies off their bellies, they would kick each other by accident. Jamie heard them squeal and grunt. They were skinny, tired-looking beasts. They had coats matted with mud. Their hooves turned up at the toes.

Jamie peered into one of these pens. Then he heard someone whisper something to him. He looked around to see who had spoken. There was no one standing nearby. He looked back at the dirty ponies. Then he heard the voice again. This time he heard it say clearly, "Please buy me. I need your help."

Startled, Jamie began to move away. He thought that someone was joking with him. Then he noticed a shabby gray pony sticking his nose through the boards. Jamie reached out to pat the nose.

"That's right. I'm really quite nice," Jamie heard. "Just bid on number 87."

Jamie couldn't believe his ears. He turned all the way around twice. Then he climbed to the top of the pen. He peered down inside to make sure no one was hiding among the ponies. Number 87 was watching him.

He really wouldn't be too bad looking if someone fed and groomed him, thought Jamie. The pony kept watching him. He arched his thin neck. Jamie knew he had to have the pony.

By the side of the auction ring Mr. Hill nudged Jamie several times when the sleek fat ponies were led through. Jamie shook his head "no" to each one. Then he saw the gray coat and white mane and tail of number 87.

"Dad, I'm going to bid on this one," he announced.

Jamie watched his father's face take on its I-don't-approve look. "That one is so thin. He looks like no one's ever taken care of him. And look at his hooves, so curled up at the toes. He may never be able to walk right."

"But I want him, Dad! I'll fix him up!"

"Why that one? You know I'll buy you a much better pony," his dad said.

The auctioneer was saying, "Ninety, ninety, who'll gi' me ninety?"

Then . . . "Eighty, eighty . . ."

"No, Dad, I don't want any other pony. Please! He'll be sold. Please may I bid on him?" Jamie pleaded.

"See, no one else is bidding. No one else is foolish enough to want that sorry-looking pony," said Jamie's dad firmly.

"Seventy, seventy . . . anyone gi' me seventy?"

"I've seen a big man in a straw hat bid on the lame and thin ones," said Jamie.

"Yes," said his dad, "that would be the man from the slaughter house."

"How 'bout sixty . . . sixty?" the auctioneer barked.

"Sixty!" called a man from the stands.

Jamie glanced across the ring at the bidder. It was the man in the straw hat! Jamie's face felt hot. His heart was pounding. He must save this pony.

"Sixty-five!" he yelled.

His dad just looked at him and shook his head.

"Sixty-five once, sixty-five twice ... SOLD to the little blond boy for sixty-five dollars."

Jamie saw number 87 wink at him as the pony was taken from the ring.

2

The five hundred-acre Foothill Ranch was nestled in the foothills of a mountain range. There were not many trees in that section of the Southwest, but grass grew well. It was good country for horses and cattle. Most folks in the area, like the Hill family, made a living raising cattle.

Ever since Jamie's new pony arrived, Jamie had spent his time in the barn. Today Jamie was carefully trying to unwrap the long white mane from clumps of burrs which were matting it together.

His dad came rushing into the barn. "When will you start listening to me?" asked Mr. Hill as he grabbed his saddle from a rack and walked into the stall of a big buckskin horse.

"If you had listened to me at the auction, you

13

would now have a pony you could ride. All you have is that sore-footed bag of bones. Right now I could use another cowboy. But what use is a cowboy if he can't ride his horse?"

Mr. Hill gave the girth a final check, sprang into the saddle and loped his horse out of the barnyard.

Jamie wanted to stick up for his pony. But there was no doubt the animal was still skinny and very lame.

Jamie finished the mane and began brushing his pony. "You won't be a bag of bones for long," Jamie said out loud. He ran his hand over the pony's side. The hair was getting sleek. There was a hint of a shine like gray steel. The ribs weren't sticking out too badly anymore.

"I guess all the hay and oats you've been eating have done you some good," he told the pony.

Jamie stared at the pony's feet, still curled up at the toes.

Jamie grabbed the hoof nippers. "Dad's not here to help me with your hooves today. So I've got to fix you up by myself."

He'd never trimmed a hoof before, but he'd

watched his dad many times. The nippers were heavy. He tried to decide exactly where on the hoof he should make his first cut. He knew that if he cut too much, the hoof would bleed. He squeezed the handles of the nippers together while he held the pony's hoof tightly between his knees. He squeezed the nippers harder. Sweat began to break out on his face and back. Finally, SNAP! A piece of hoof neatly broke off. Jamie wiped his face on his shirt while he let the pony put his hoof down.

"This job is harder than I figured," said Jamie to the pony.

He felt like quitting and asking his dad to help when he got home. But after thinking about it for a minute, he grabbed the nippers and picked up the pony's hoof again.

3

Weeks passed and Jamie was feeling more and more puzzled. His pony ate, drank, closed his eyes when brushed, but didn't talk. While he shoveled the soiled bedding into the wheelbarrow, Jamie complained aloud to his pony.

"I'm beginning to think that there really was someone at the auction who played a trick on me. I was sure dumb to bid on you. Dad was right all along. If I had bid on one of those good ponies, I'd have been riding in the hills weeks ago."

With his pitchfork, he threw the last mess of soggy bedding on top of the wheelbarrow.

"I was sure dumb," he sighed. "I've been stuck here in the barn taking care of you as if you were king and I was your slave . . . And you've never even

said 'thank you,' " he added as he wheeled the load of bedding out the barn door. He shoved the wheelbarrow as high up the side of the manure pile as he could and tipped out his load.

"Thank you, Jamie," he heard from the barn.

"Who's here?" he demanded to the darkest corner. Nobody answered. Jamie looked at his pony. The pony winked. "You do talk!" Jamie breathed half to himself.

"Of course," the pony said flatly.

"What's your name?" asked Jamie.

"My name's Whimsy."

"But why have you waited so long to talk to me again?" Jamie asked.

"Didn't have anything to say," said Whimsy. He switched his tail at a fly which was looking for a tender place on his back.

Jamie stared at his pony. He looked like just a regular pony, standing in the stall swatting flies. "Why . . . how . . . Whimsy . . . can . . . can you talk?" Jamie stammered, getting more and more excited.

"Can your mother and father talk?" Whimsy asked.

"Sure," answered Jamie.

"So you talk too, right?" asked Whimsy.

"Sure," said Jamie.

"Well, there you have it, you see?"

"No, I don't see!" protested Jamie. "I'm a person. I'm supposed to talk. You're just a pony!"

The pony's ears flicked back. His straight lined horse-face almost looked offended. "I am not *just* a pony. You'll see."

Whimsy sniffed the ground. He bent his legs and gracefully let himself settle down on top of the fresh straw in his stall. He closed his eyes.

"Oh, come on! Don't go to sleep!" begged Jamie. "Please tell me more."

Whimsy blinked sleepily at him. He began to breathe the slow peaceful breaths of sleep.

4

The pony's talking made Jamie more curious than ever. Every time he did chores or visited the barnyard he'd try to get the pony to talk. But Whimsy was as stubborn about talking as the average pony can be about being ridden.

Jamie even tried to trick Whimsy into speech. Once he carried the water bucket into the barn, put it down on the floor and went out to feed the cattle. He pretended to forget to place the water where Whimsy could reach it. Jamie listened to noises in the barn while he scooped oats into the cattle feeder. But all he heard was snorting and kicking from the barn. He didn't hear the words, "You forgot my water," as he hoped to hear. Pretty soon Mr. Hill stuck his head out of the hayloft door and yelled for Jamie to "Go stop that worthless pony from wrecking the barn!"

"Whimsy, you didn't have to kick your stall apart just 'cause I forgot your water. All you had to do was tell me. I only wanted you to talk to me again," said Jamie sadly, as he walked outside.

School would be starting soon and he wouldn't have as much time to spend with his pony. At the thought of school Jamie turned back toward the barn and sat, head in hands, on a hay bale. Jack Rodgers would be in school. He was older than Jamie and had a big black pony. He always teased the younger boys about being too little to have ponies of their own. Jack's pony was almost horse size. He was always bragging about how his pony could work cattle almost as well as the ranch hands' cow horses. Jack lived on a ranch two miles down the gravel road toward town. He was a neighbor. That meant Jamie would have to ride ten miles to and from school listening to Jack brag and tease. The worst part about it would be that his dad had told Mr. Rodgers about the auction and Whimsy.

Jamie never let things worry him for long,

though. He knew he didn't want to face Jack's teasing on the school bus. He knew the only way to stop it would be to be riding Whimsy by the time school started. "Maybe I'll even ride him down the road, past the Rodgers' ranch a time or two. Then Jack can see with his own eyes that I have a pony as good as any," decided Jamie. He smiled, thinking about his idea.

"Okay, Whimsy, this is it," announced Jamie as he marched into the stall carrying a saddle and bridle. Whimsy sniffed the saddle for a moment and then took a big taste of one of the latigo straps. "You donkey!" Jamie yelled, snatching the saddle out of Whimsy's reach. "Now, how am I going to tie stuff like my jacket to the back of my saddle! I thought you were supposed to be smart." He almost slapped the pony on the neck, but caught himself before he let his hand fall. He had a funny feeling that it would be more like slapping a person than an animal.

Jamie carefully checked the pony's feet. Then he tacked up Whimsy and led him out of the barn. Feeling somewhat nervous, Jamie mounted the

pony. He wasn't really sure Whimsy's feet were well enough to be ridden. Also, even though the pony was smart enough to talk, did he know he wasn't supposed to buck? Since Whimsy ate the latigo strap, Jamie wasn't so sure about how much the pony knew.

Whimsy didn't buck. He didn't tremble like a pony that had never been ridden. He didn't dance excitedly around the barnyard like a pony that had been badly trained. He didn't move.

Jamie squeezed Whimsy's sides with his lower legs. He squeezed harder. He gently kicked the pony's ribs with his heels. Then he kicked harder. He pulled Whimsy's head around almost to his knee, to get him off balance enough to move a foot. Whimsy stood still and flicked his ears back and forth, mostly back. "Get going, you short-eared cousin to a mule, you!" yelled Jamie finally.

Whimsy stepped smartly forward, causing Jamie to lose his balance. By this time he wasn't really expecting the pony to move. Jamie was about to scold Whimsy for being a wise guy, when he thought that maybe Whimsy just didn't understand. Every

horse Jamie had ever ridden would go if he squeezed with his legs or kicked with his heels. Jamie decided that he'd just have to tell this stubborn pony what to do.

"Trot," said Jamie, and off they went trotting around the barnyard. Suddenly Jamie felt happier than he'd ever felt. The air, crisp with the coming fall, blew through his hair. They went through the gate, into the open meadow. "Lope, please," said Jamie softly. Whimsy broke into an easy lope. Then he began to run faster and faster across the meadow. When they reached the far fence that enclosed the eighty-acre field Whimsy skidded to a snorting stop.

"Whimsy, that was great!" exclaimed Jamie.

"Yeah!" Whimsy puffed, too excited to feel stubborn about talking. "I forgot what fun a good gallop is!"

As they turned back toward the ranch, Whimsy took small, slow steps. "Are you tired?" Jamie asked. Whimsy didn't answer. He laid his ears back and Jamie heard his breath come in short quick gasps.

"Whoa!" Jamie jumped off. Something was wrong. "Let me see you walk," he ordered.

Slowly Whimsy stepped forward. His head bobbed up and down. His eyes squinted. "Oh, no! You're lame again! I should have known better," groaned Jamie. "Why did I ever let you gallop? It was just too much. Whimsy, why didn't you tell me your feet hurt?" demanded Jamie.

"I didn't realize they hurt until we stopped."

"Now what shall we do?" asked Jamie.

"You can't ride me," said Whimsy.

"I know that. I didn't mean now. I meant what can I tell Dad?" Jamie drooped. "And what about Jack Rodgers on the bus?"

Jamie looked so worried it made Whimsy feel almost as bad to look at the boy as it did to walk on his sore feet. So to cheer Jamie up as well as he could, Whimsy talked to Jamie the whole way home.

5

Whimsy told Jamie why he wasn't *just* a pony. He was one of the wild horses. His mother had been a pack pony until she was taken by the wild stallion to run with the herd. The wild horses roamed the western plains, but they had trouble finding land to live on. Ranchers wanted more and more land for their cattle to graze on. So the ranchers chased wild horses in jeeps and airplanes, and killed them. How the horses actually learned to talk, Whimsy wasn't sure. He just knew that when he was born his parents taught him both the language of horses and of men. He often heard his parents speak of leading the wild horses to a safe place. They wanted a place where they could live in peace and still find enough food to eat.

One spring the horses left the mountains to see if they could find such a place. But the men in jeeps spotted the herd. After a long, cruel chase, Whimsy's father saw that his mares and foals were getting tired. He knew he had to do something or they'd all be killed. So he gave the order to split up. Half the herd was to follow him, the other half was to follow Whimsy's mom. For an instant Whimsy didn't know if he should follow his mom or his dad. As he slowed down to think, he heard something hiss through the air. A rope tightened around his neck. Another rope snagged his hind legs as he kicked out in anger. He fell. A man tied the ropes. He was left alone. He fought and fell until he lay in a helpless heap.

Later a jeep came by. A man untied the rope on Whimsy's legs and hitched the neck rope to the jeep's bumper. Whimsy heard the men saying that they had lost half the herd. The rest of them had been driven into a catch pen which had been hidden in the hills. Whimsy felt sick wondering which bunch had been caught. He pictured the wild horses trying to batter their way out of the fence with the last of their strength.

Whimsy was kept locked in a dark stall in a barn. Then he was finally brought to the auction to be sold.

"I've got to find out what happened to the herd and help my father finish his job of bringing the wild ones to safety. I need your help," finished Whimsy as they neared the barnyard.

"What can I do?" asked Jamie.

But Whimsy would say no more that day.

6

When school began, Whimsy's feet were still healing. He looked fine while he was walking or grazing. But the few times Jamie slipped gently onto his back, the pony would falter and stumble. Just as Jamie had feared, Jack began to taunt him each day on the school bus.

"Heard ya got a pony ya can't ride! You scared of him?" sneered Jack.

"No. I've ridden him, only he's lame now," Jamie replied.

"Yeah, heard ya bought him that way," Jack continued.

"He got better. Only he got sore again when I rode him too fast," protested Jamie.

"How fast did ya ride? . . . A fast walk?"

Nothing Jamie said seemed good enough for Jack, so Jamie just kept quiet.

Jack began to brag. He told of how he helped his dad ride fence lines and chase down stray calves all summer. He told of how one weekend he rode his pony in a barrel race. He told of another weekend when they went out hunting wild horses.

"That's more than you little kids, especially ones who buy lame ponies, will ever be able to do," Jack said. He ended his speech as the bus pulled up to his driveway.

Through the cloud of dust the bus left behind on the gravel road, Jamie saw Jack vault the fence and take off running. As the bus rounded a curve he could still see the distant figure moving swiftly across the field. But this time he was mounted Indian-style on the back of his sleek black pony.

When Jamie got home he dumped his books on the kitchen table and rushed out the back door as he headed toward the barn. I hate Jack Rodgers, he muttered.

Jamie patted Whimsy. He turned him loose on the front lawn to eat grass. He'd been doing that every afternoon since school began. Seeing Whimsy grazing near the house made doing homework a tiny bit easier.

About an hour later, Jamie was in his room wrestling with a math problem. Suddenly he heard a yell, a crash and pounding hooves. He ran out on the porch. He caught a glimpse of Whimsy's tail as it vanished into the open barn. There was his mother standing in the midst of broken plants and pottery. Dirt was scattered all over the porch. His mom's arm was wrapped in a towel.

"What happened, Mom?" Jamie asked.

"That pony of yours had his head over the railing with half of my ivy plant in his mouth. I yelled. When he ran, he must have still had a hold of that ivy," said Jamie's mother.

"But what happened to all those other plants? Why's your arm in a towel?" asked Jamie.

"The ivy was in a big pot. It fell and knocked all the plants off the lower shelves. I burned my arm," Jamie's mother said.

"On the plants?" he snickered.

"Don't be funny," she said. "On the oven. I came

out here to get some of my aloe plant to rub on it. But my aloe seems to be crushed beneath that fern."

Jamie picked up the aloe. Chunks of earth clung to the greenish juice which oozed from the battered plant.

"So much for that one," said Jamie's mom. She went back to the kitchen, leaving Jamie to sweep and shovel the porch clean.

7

The sound of autumn leaves crackled in the crisp air. Gone were the summer sounds of the night insects and the whippoorwill. Jamie was asleep. His window was open in spite of a chilly breeze. He could sleep better when he could hear the night sounds. Jamie was dreaming of riding the ridges on his pony. Their trail took them far away from chores and school and Jack Rodgers. His dream was of campfires and sleeping under the stars. Whimsy was munching close by. His hand pushed Whimsy's velvet nose away from his cheek. "Go eat grass, Whimsy. Don't bother me," he said in his sleep. The soft nuzzling continued and his dream hand could not make it stop.

"Come with me!" he heard in the dark. Jamie

squinted his drowsy eyes toward the window. He saw the head and neck of his pony. Whimsy was stretched into the room as far as he could reach.

"Grab your jacket and come," Whimsy commanded. Jamie climbed out of bed. He grabbed his jacket off the hook behind the door and climbed out the window onto Whimsy's fat back.

The hint of frost in the air made him wish he'd put something on his bare feet. But the pony was warm. As they loped, Jamie snuggled against the pony's fuzzy fall coat. "Where are we going?" whispered Jamie in the pony's ear.

"I shouldn't have spoiled your mother's plants. We're off to find her a new aloe and maybe I can find news of my parents, too."

"But your feet . . . Are they all right?" Jamie asked.

"They feel okay now. I'll be more careful this time," snorted Whimsy.

They crossed moonlit meadows and trotted over tree-dotted hills. They stopped whenever they met a night creature. The pony neighed to an owl who answered with a series of hoots. Even the scurrying lizards seemed to have something to say to Whimsy. Their trail took them into high country that Jamie had never seen before. At first he was awed by huge jags of rock, shadowed before moonlit clouds. They had left the meadow grass, trees and ranch lights in the valleys below them. The footing became more slippery. Jamie realized that they were traveling through dangerous country where he was not allowed to ride.

Whimsy seemed to have sensed his nervousness. The pony turned down the trail toward home. "Are we going back now?" asked Jamie.

"Yes, it's getting late. Besides, now I've got a better idea about where my parents may be."

"What about Mom's aloe?"

"Oh, I almost forgot. There should be some on the south side of one of these hills. It would be in a place where it would be sunny if it were day." Whimsy snorted a few times and Jamie saw a shadowy shape of what looked like a horned toad. "There's your aloe!" announced Whimsy, stopping.

Jamie slid off, flinching as his feet touched cold rocks. "At least I didn't step on a cactus," he sighed

sleepily. He dug up the little plant with his pocket knife. He gently place it in his pocket and climbed back on the pony.

Whimsy felt warm and comfy. Jamie took a deep breath and realized how tired he was. He buried his face deeper into the pony's white mane and clung on tight.

When he woke up, the sun was shining on him through the window of his own room.

As soon as his memory of the night returned, Jamie looked out the window. He saw Whimsy in the pasture. Eating as always, Jamie thought. It must have been a dream.

As he swung his legs to the floor something felt itchy on the seat of his pajamas. Jamie rubbed his eyes. It was pony hair! It must have really happened! While he stared at the short gray hairs, he thought he could remember stumbling into bed as dawn began to color the sky.

"My jacket!" he cried. He jumped up. There it was in a heap on the floor. He thrust his hand into the pocket. The aloe was there!

"Jamie, breakfast!" It was his mother calling

from the kitchen. He folded his jacket carefully around the plant, dressed and headed for the kitchen.

"You look tired, dear," said Jamie's mom. "Your father wanted to wake you an hour ago for chores. But I was worried you might not be feeling well. You never sleep this late. Let me feel your forehead."

"Hey, Mom, I feel okay," he said absently. He thought about how to tell his mom and dad about the plant and his adventure. No, they won't believe me, he thought to himself. Just like I know they won't believe that Whimsy talks. Besides, what if they do believe me? They'd forbid me to go again... if there is another time. So all he said out loud was, "I guess I'm just tired from a rough week at school." Later he would figure out how to explain the new aloe plant. Right now all he wanted to do was eat.

8

The school bus would be at the bottom of the driveway in five minutes. Jamie still had to feed Whimsy. He always saved that chore for last. That way if he had extra time, he could spend it with his pony. Today he had to hurry, but he wanted to talk to Whimsy.

"I'm having a tough time explaining to Mom and Dad about our ride the other night. It would sure make it easier on me if you would talk to them. If they could just hear you say anything at all, I know they'd understand."

"Would they?" asked Whimsy through a mouthful of oats. He chewed for a minute. "I may not know everything about humans—but I do know enough not to talk to adults."

47

"But why?" asked Jamie.

"They would put me in a zoo or a circus or on T.V. or send me away to be studied. Nope, I'll never talk to an adult."

"My folks wouldn't do anything like that!"

"I'm not about to find out." Whimsy grabbed another mouthful.

Jamie heard the motor of the school bus in the distance. He had to go.

"You riding that plug, yet?" Jack yelled from the back of the school bus. Jamie had ignored Jack all last week. But after the weekend's midnight adventure he now had something to talk about. He sat down across the aisle from Jack.

"I rode Whimsy the other night," he said.

"Night? You ashamed to let anyone see you?" challenged Jack.

"We were looking for wild horses."

"Bull!" bellowed Jack. "You're crazy! You can't track wild horses at night. Besides, wild horses aren't worth anything unless they're dead!"

"Oh, yeah?" said Jamie. "I bet you I can show you wild horses."

"I still say you're crazy! You're dreamin' if you think you could come even close to a bunch of wild horses."

The school bus stopped. Jack and Jamie jumped out.

"I am not crazy!" yelled Jamie. "You be at my place tonight at midnight and I'll prove it to you!"

"Oh, no, now what have I done?" said Jamie to himself as the bus pulled away. But since he couldn't swallow his words, he began to imagine what a midnight ride with Jack would be like. And what will Whimsy say about it? he thought.

9

That night Jamie didn't wait for Whimsy to come get him. He was nervous and excited when he went to bed. He didn't even get undressed. As soon as the house was quiet he climbed out the window and headed for the barn. In the dark he tacked some old feed sacks over the barn windows which could be seen from the house. He got his face snagged in cobwebs as he climbed into mangers and on hay bales to reach the windows. Finally done, he cautiously turned on the light. Sleepy-eyed animals blinked. Whimsy snorted.

"Couldn't you have brushed me in the dark just as easily as done that nasty job?" asked Whimsy from his stall.

"I don't think Jack will be here for another hour

51

and a half. I didn't feel like sitting in the dark all that time," said Jamie.

"Jack! Isn't that the kid you don't like? What's he doing coming here?" asked Whimsy.

"I told Jack we were going to find the wild horses tonight. He didn't believe we could find them. Since he always picks on me, I had to prove to him we could find the horses. I didn't mean to invite him along. It just sort of happened. Maybe having him along won't be too awful," Jamie ended rather lamely.

Whimsy had as angry a look as a pony could have. His ears flicked back and forth and his tail twitched. "I should tell you we won't go tonight. But I do want to find the herd. I should leave you here and go myself," said Whimsy, almost to himself. "But I need you to open gates, even if you're not useful for much else," he snorted.

"Oh, Whimsy, I'm sorry. I didn't mean to make you mad. Have a carrot." Jamie took a handful of carrot sticks out of his pocket. Jamie sat on the hay and munched, too. Despite the winter night, the barn was warm with the body heat from the six other horses and two cows that were stabled there. The only sounds were the munching of carrots and hooves lazily stepping on straw bedding.

After five or six carrot sticks Whimsy didn't look so mad any more. Jamie nestled more comfortably into the hay. Suddenly the big buckskin threw up his head and whinnied. There was the sound of horse hooves, then an answering whinny from outside.

"We haven't even started yet, and that friend of yours is already bringing trouble. His loudmouthed pony is going to wake your folks," Whimsy grumbled.

Jack's head appeared at the barn door. He led his black pony inside. "Kid, I think you're nuts. It's black as a cave out there tonight. I don't know how you think you'll ever find anything, let alone wild horses, on a night like this. It was hard enough just getting here," he admitted. "I had to go by the road. It was too dark to gallop across the fields."

Jamie was saddling and bridling Whimsy. "We can do it, you'll see," he said.

"I still think you're crazy. I wouldn't have come at

54

all except it's going to be funny to see you make a fool of yourself," laughed Jack.

Whimsy was liking this noisy human less and less. He was mad at Jamie for having Jack there. Jamie was about to lead Whimsy out of the barn. Whimsy stopped in front of Jack and looked him in the eye.

"You mount up and shut up. Jamie and I know exactly what we are doing. Everything will be fine as long as you don't ruin it with your mouth. You ar.d your pony will do what I say, or you won't come." Then Whimsy looked at Jamie. "Just maybe he'll come in handy."

Jamie was trying hard to hold back a smile.

Jack was standing in the center of the barn, his mouth flapping but no sound was coming out. He looked from Whimsy to Jamie and back to Whimsy.

"Come on, we've wasted enough time already," said Whimsy, giving Jamie a gentle nudge.

Jamie switched off the light, mounted, and he and Whimsy headed westward across the fields.

A few minutes later, Jack rode up. "Hey," he chuckled, "that's a pretty good trick you and that

pony can do. It's just like they do on T.V. You almost had me fooled."

"It's no trick," said Whimsy. "I can talk better than you."

Whimsy's voice certainly sounds different than Jamie's, thought Jack. But he still couldn't believe it. "Jamie, you get off and stay here. I'll lead your pony across the field. If he doesn't talk without you nearby to make him—I'll owe you somethin' for trying to make a fool of me."

"Jack, we have things to do . . ." Jamie began.

"Let's get this over with," said Whimsy. "If this is what it takes to get this kid to keep quiet, I'm all for it."

Jamie dismounted. Jack reached for Whimsy's bridle reins, but Jamie looped them around the saddle horn. "He'll go with you without you pulling him. He's the one who wanted to go along with your dumb idea, not me."

Jamie watched Jack move off with Whimsy, to be swallowed by the dark night. Jamie knew Whimsy would find him again. But standing alone in the starless, cold night was spooky.

"Hey, Jamie, can ya hear me?" Jamie heard Jack's distant voice.

"I hear you!" Jamie yelled.

Shortly he heard hoof beats. The ponies and Jack reappeared.

"He does talk," Jack croaked. "I can't believe it."

"Now, if you want to come with us, keep quiet and no more fooling around," commanded Whimsy.

10

Jamie mounted Whimsy and Jack climbed back onto his pony. The ponies headed west at a trot.

After they went through the last ranch gate, their pace had to slow from a jog trot to a walk. Once in a while a slip of the moon would peek from behind the clouds.

Jack followed along in silence. There were many questions he wanted to ask. But he was still too startled to say anything. Along with the pony being able to talk, the darkness of the night made the whole adventure seem unreal.

Jack prided himself on knowing every inch of the nearby hills. But he didn't know where he was now. They could be anywhere, for all he knew. For almost the first time in his life, he was afraid to say a thing. He was afraid that if he made this strange pony angry he'd find himself left alone in an unknown canyon miles from anywhere he knew. He kept his eyes glued on Whimsy's white tail. Many minutes would pass and that white tail was all that Jack could see.

Jamie knew that they were traveling along the same route they had taken the time before. They were crossing the grass-covered hills.

Then they entered a dry riverbed. The gravel crunched beneath their hooves. They were climbing now. As the trail became steeper, it began to wind around boulders. The boulders were so close together that Jamie could reach out and touch them with his hand. Every once in a while Jamie would ask Whimsy to stop. He would listen to make sure Jack's pony was still behind.

After a sudden turn, the trail opened into a steep-walled canyon. The clouds were breaking up. The boys could see the shapes of rocks and trees on the cliffs far above them. They turned to the side and stopped by a small waterfall. Jack's pony began slurping water. They heard another noise, a faint

sound in the distance. It was the snorting of horses.

"Jamie, we found them!" whispered Jack, amazed.

"Hush," whispered Whimsy. "Jamie, get off and stay here with Jack until I get back. And keep quiet, please."

Jack dismounted alongside Jamie. He hitched his pony to a tree and sat down next to Jamie on a rock. They strained their eyes and ears to the far side of the canyon trying to discover what was happening. Jamie had a sinking feeling in the pit of his stomach that Whimsy wouldn't be coming back. Perhaps that's why he said Jack may be useful . . . to bring me home, worried Jamie. Then he whispered out loud, "Why do you suppose Whimsy wanted us to wait here?"

"So the horses won't hear us," whispered Jack. "Now, hush, we're supposed to be quiet." They waited and waited. Jamie became more and more worried. If Whimsy didn't return, how could they find their way home?

After what seemed like hours, they saw Whimsy's white mane jogging toward them. A huge, light gray horse was at his side. The gray reared and whirled away as soon as he saw the boys. Whimsy kept coming.

Jamie jumped up and hugged Whimsy around the neck. "Tell us what happened," he whispered.

"The gray horse is my father," explained Whimsy excitedly. "The herd has been having trouble finding water. More and more of their water holes are being fenced in. Here they have water but no grass. They are not getting by very well. They need help. But you have to promise that no one will hurt them."

"Okay," said Jamie eagerly. "What'll we do?"

"We'll lead the herd to the hills behind your ranch," Whimsy told him. "They'll stay there for a day or so until we get them through to the game refuge. Then the horses will be safe. Come on." Then Whimsy turned to Jack.

"I've told them I had two boys with me. They won't be scared of you as long as you're quiet. You stay here as Jamie and I lead out. When all the horses go past, you follow along behind. It will be your job to make sure none of the little ones stray off," said Whimsy.

"Those foals need you," he added. "On our way here there were coyotes all over the place. They'll smell you and stay out of sight even if a foal does stray. And another thing, it's so dark it will be hard for my father to watch over all the horses by himself."

"Oh... Okay," said Jack as he reined in his pony.

In order to follow Whimsy through the narrow mouth of the canyon, mares, foals, yearlings and young stallions had to pass by close to where Jack was standing. Each one of them sidestepped in alarm as they spied him through the darkness. Close up the horses looked worn and scraggly to Jack. They didn't look like he had pictured them. With their large brown eyes, soft little muzzles, and long wobbly legs, the foals looked like they needed to be protected. When the last of them shied past him, Jack urged his black pony forward and followed along behind.

He couldn't see Jamie and Whimsy. They were too far ahead and it was still dark. Often the gray stallion would trot by as he made his rounds back and forth keeping watch over the herd. I sure hope these horses don't decide to split up or go off on their own, Jack worried. The country seemed strange and wild to him. He felt lonely and scared. Sometimes he couldn't see any of the horses. If he lost them, would his pony know the way home? Fearfully, Jack urged his pony close to the wild horses.

Suddenly, the gray stallion loomed in front of him. The stallion reared and lunged. Jack's pony jerked aside and Jack felt himself sliding from the saddle.

If I fall now, the stallion will trample me! Jack muttered. He grabbed the pony's mane. Somehow he managed to hang on as the pony lurched again. Then the pony stood trembling, but still. The gray stallion stood and seemed to stare as if warning them to keep away.

Jack waited until the stallion disappeared in the darkness. Then he rode forward again.

At last Whimsy led the herd back to Foothill Ranch. The sun was almost up. They found a meadow between some hills. The meadow was hidden enough from view that the horses should be

safe as long as they stayed put. Whimsy snorted and whinnied to the wild ones. Some of the horses put their heads down and began hungrily cropping grass.

Jamie signaled for Jack to come on ahead. "Looks like we'll need some hay for them," said Jack as he caught up. "If they stay in that meadow for more than a day they'll eat that dry grass down to nothing."

"I'll see if I can get some hay to them," said Jamie. "You have any idea about how we can get them through that fifty-mile stretch of fenced ranchland?"

"Leave that to me," offered Jack. "My dad knows a lot of people. Even if he doesn't like the wild horses, he'll help us out some, just because I ask him."

"Hey, thanks, Jack. But are you sure your dad won't want to hurt the horses?"

"Not if I ask him to help. Besides, I won't tell him where they are."

"We'll have to keep folks from finding these horses in the next few days," stated Jamie.

"If they don't go raiding anyone's saddle stock, no one should know they're here. Not many folks are riding out this way this time of year," Jack said. "What about getting permission from the game refuge people? We can't take the horses there without permission."

"I'll phone them today," called Jamie. He turned Whimsy through a gate into the fields of Foothill Ranch. "I've got to run. If I don't get into my room before Mom and Dad get up, I'll have all kinds of explaining to do. Bye!"

"Bye! See ya on the bus," Jack called to him.

"The bus! I'd forgotten it's Friday today! Ugh!" Jamie and Whimsy galloped off.

Jack galloped past where Jamie turned. He headed south. He had a longer way to go before sunup, but he wasn't worried. He was smiling and whistling to himself. He'd tell his dad about the adventure. In fact, he had a lot to tell his dad. He'd had the most exciting adventure ever. And he had even made a friend.

Once in the barn, Jamie took Whimsy's saddle off and rubbed him down. "I'll be out soon and give you your feed and water."

"Take your time," answered Whimsy. "I need a nap."

Jamie slipped into the window of his own room. He had just enough time to change before he heard his mother calling, "Breakfast's ready!"

11

"Hi!" called Jack as Jamie got on the bus. They sat together and talked together in low voices all the way to school. The other kids on the bus could hardly believe it.

After school Jamie spent almost an hour talking on the phone. Then he went to talk things over with his parents. He found them in the kitchen going over the bookkeeping.

"Jack and I will need your help tomorrow," he announced. "We've got this herd of wild horses out in the hills. The forest rangers in the game refuge north of here said that if we could get the horses there, they'd protect them like they do the wild deer and elk."

"Whoa, there," said his dad. "What wild horses?"

It took Jamie quite a while to explain about how and why he and Jack were mixed up in wild horses at all. Jamie had been practicing his speech in his mind all afternoon. He managed a good explanation, telling just enough of the truth without telling his folks that Whimsy could talk.

"Well," said his dad. "I wish you had told me some of this before. I'm not really such a hard guy to get along with that you have to keep everything a secret. You've done a lot of work on this crazy project. I'll help you out. How about you, Mom?"

"You know, it does sound like fun, driving wild horses across country. I haven't gone on an overnight ride for years. And I suppose you'll need a hand. Count me in," said Jamie's mom.

"When did you say we are going?" asked his dad.

"Tomorrow!" cried Jamie. "Oh, thanks! I've got to go tell . . . uh, I mean check on Whimsy." Jamie ran out the door and to the barn.

12

At sunup the next morning Jack and Mr. Rodgers rode up the driveway of Foothill Ranch. Jamie's mom mounted her bay mare. Jamie had Whimsy tacked up. Jamie was tying his sleeping bag on the back of his saddle with baling twine. His dad checked the straps on the pack horse one more time, and they were all ready.

The five riders headed toward the meadow in the hills. The boys were out front. "I hope the horses haven't had a notion to wander off," said Jack.

"They'll be there," Jamie assured him.

Whimsy nodded his head.

The horses were there. A shrill whinny rang across the hills as the five riders rode near. They stopped about one-half mile from the meadow.

"You all stay here," Jamie told the others. "Jack and I will lead them out."

"But, Son," said Mr. Hill. "Even though you did well finding these horses the other night, don't forget they are not tame saddle stock. If you ride into that meadow they'll spook. We should sneak up behind them. That stallion sounds uneasy already."

"Dad, these . . . these aren't the usual wild horses. Leave this to me."

Jamie's dad was about to argue. "Don't forget this project belongs to the boys," cautioned Jamie's mom. "We are just along for the ride."

The two boys rode off. The adults sat astride their horses watching the hills. Soon Whimsy and Jamie appeared. Then came Jack on his black. Following them were a milling herd of paints, grays, bays and chestnuts. Long-legged foals frisked about. The older horses walked along quietly like cattle. The amazed adults moved their horses along behind the last of the mares.

Suddenly a gray figure exploded in a series of bucks and leaps between the wild mares and the humans on their horses. The stallion, with his ears back and his hindquarters swinging, threatened the people. He snorted angrily. Then he calmed down as the riders drew back further. He continued to trot back and forth between his mares and the adults during the whole ride. He would lay his ears back and buck whenever the adults came close.

Glancing back, Jamie wondered why the stallion hadn't behaved quite that way the other night. Perhaps he doesn't trust the adults, Jamie thought. Whatever the reason, at least the herd was now moving north to a new and safe home.

It was one of those glorious southwestern winter days. The air was cool enough for the group to wear warm jackets, but the sun was warm on their hands and faces. They stopped for lunch. The boys made a little campfire in a stony spot by the bank of the brook. They ate sandwiches, and Jamie's mom fixed coffee and hot chocolate.

His dad and Mr. Rodgers couldn't understand why the wild horses were grazing peacefully not far from the saddle horses. Like before, the wild ones were not galloping off.

"I still don't understand it," Jamie's dad was saying. "I've never seen anything like it. Wild horses never let humans near them. There's something very strange about this. There's something you're not telling me, Jamie."

Just then, Whimsy gave a loud snort and raced off toward the gray stallion.

"Now, there goes your fool pony," grumbled Jamie's dad. "Why didn't you hobble him? We'll likely lose the whole herd if we try to catch him. You'll just have to ride behind me."

Jamie couldn't believe that Whimsy would desert him. He stood looking off where Whimsy and his father were grazing.

By the time the lunch things were all packed and everyone was saddled up, Whimsy was back. Gratefully, Jamie tacked up. They started off again with the wild horses. The gray stallion took his place between the herd and the humans following behind. They traveled northward, through pastures, down ranch lanes, through gates and past grazing cattle. Once in a while they'd see ranchers out fixing fence or hauling hay in pickup trucks. They would wave

and the ranchers would stare. Jamie guessed that none of them had really believed it when they heard two boys were going to drive a herd of wild horses through their places.

13

The next day it began to snow. By late afternoon, the boys led the wild horses onto the game refuge lands. As they trailed past the rangers' head-quarters, a ranger waved. He mounted his horse and rode with them to the wild herd's new home. They rode out on a ridge overlooking rolling prairie land. The hills were dotted with trees and in the distance was a fringe of mountains. It was hard to tell how good the grass was under the inch of snow which had fallen. But the ranger told them that there would be enough grass for the horses.

Whimsy snorted and whinnied to the gray stal-lion. The gray galloped away in front of the herd. The wild ones burst away in a joyful scrambling race down the slippery slope. They ran out onto the low

snow-covered hills.

"It's eerie," said the ranger. "It's just like they understood what was going on. Did you drug those horses to trail them so easily?" the ranger asked as they turned away.

"Nope," Jack answered, smiling.

All the way back to headquarters the ranger kept wondering how wild horses could let themselves be herded so calmly. A big blue cattle truck was waiting for them in front of ranger headquarters. Jack's dad had told one of his ranch hands to come with the truck and pick them up that evening so the boys would get home in time for school Monday.

Whimsy and the saddle horses were loaded into the truck. The adults rode in the cab. Jamie and Jack rode in the space over the cab. They lay on their stomachs looking back at the horses.

"That was the best ride I've ever been on in my life. Thanks, Whimsy," said Jamie.

"I should thank you!" said Whimsy softly under the noise of the truck engine.

14

A week had gone by and everyone seemed to be over the excitement of the wild horse adventure. Jamie went to the barn one morning to feed Whimsy. As he entered the barn he had a strange feeling. Then he saw the empty stall. Whimsy was gone. Maybe he was so thirsty he couldn't wait for me, thought Jamie after a moment. But he had a feeling that wasn't what had happened, and ran outside. He strained his eyes in the direction of the nearest pond. There wasn't any sign of Whimsy.

Jamie ran back to the house. "Mom! Dad! Whimsy's gone!" he cried. "Can I borrow your horse, Mom, to go look for him?"

"Gone? Well . . . I guess so . . . Okay, but be careful. My mare gets jumpy sometimes," his mom told him. "Don't worry about school today. I know how important Whimsy is to you."

"Thanks, Mom!"

"Hold on, Son. I'm coming with you," his dad called as Jamie headed for the door.

They rode through the pastures following the fencelines. They looked for breaks where the pony could have gone through. Following a fence line to the north, they found an open gate. Beyond that, along the outermost fence that separated Foothill Ranch from open rangeland, they found a break in the top wire. Jamie's dad dismounted and began to fix the break. He always carried a fence tool in a pouch on his saddle. As he picked up an end of the broken wire, he found a small patch of gray horsehide snagged on the barbs.

"Whimsy tried to jump this," his dad told Jamie.

"Oh, Dad, do you think he got hurt?" Jamie gasped.

"I can't say," said his dad. "If he was hurt badly he wouldn't have wandered off too far. Come on, we'll go around through the gate and keep looking."

They looked until dark. Finally they rode home,

tired and discouraged.

Each day after that Mr. Hill would phone the neighboring ranches to see if anyone had spotted Whimsy. "Could we call the game refuge and ask the rangers if they've seen him?" asked Jamie one day. His dad couldn't understand why the pony would head back there or even how he'd get there. But to make Jamie happy Mr. Hill finally phoned the rangers. The rangers hadn't seen any strays. They hadn't seen the herd lately either.

"The horses are still around here though," the ranger told Mr. Hill. "We've seen signs of them here and there. But the horses keep themselves pretty much out of sight."

It was hard for Jamie to face his chores without Whimsy being there. Each morning as he entered the barn, he'd make a wish that Whimsy would be standing in his stall. But each morning the stall was empty.

Every afternoon after school Jamie rode his mom's horse while looking for Whimsy. Sometimes Jack rode along. Jack invited Jamie to the indoor rodeo finals. Jack and his dad and Jamie went. The

finals and the trip to the city were fun. It took his mind off Whimsy a little, but still he missed his pony.

Then one night Jamie woke up with a start. He heard a strangely familiar snuffling sound outside. "Whimsy!" He nearly flew to the window. He threw it open and tumbled out barefooted on the frozen ground. He hugged the pony and buried a tear-streaked face in the bushy white mane.

"Oh, I'm so glad you're back!" he finally managed to say.

"I can't stay," Whimsy snorted.

There was that sinking feeling again, only worse this time. I'll get a rope and tie him, Jamie thought.

"Please don't think of tying me up," Whimsy said. "I trust you, or else I wouldn't even have come back."

"But why did you go?" Jamie asked.

"The herd still needs me. My father never did learn to understand humans as well as I do. He doesn't trust them at all. You could tell during our ride to the refuge."

"Now the herd is safe. Your job is done! You can

stay here with me," Jamie protested.

"They won't stay on the refuge unless I can keep reminding them that the rangers and tourists don't want to hurt them. They just don't trust humans and probably never will." Whimsy was quiet for a moment. "I guess that's why I left without telling you that I was going. I wasn't really sure that you wouldn't try to stop me."

"Why did you come back at all if you're just going to leave again?" Jamie sniffed.

"I wanted to tell you to get your dad to take you to the auction next month. Be sure to bid on number 50."

"But . . ." Jamie was about to argue.

"Hush! I've got a long way to go. I must leave," Whimsy said turning.

"Wait!" called Jamie. "You're not going to try to jump the barbed wire fence again, are you?"

"No, not this time. I came by road. I traveled by night and slept in the brush during the day. It worked all right. I'll go back the same way."

"Wait! Don't go yet," Jamie said, trying hard to choke back his oncoming tears. "Please . . . at least . . . let a ranger see you once you get back. I'll call them tomorrow and the next day, too, until I find out if you got back okay."

Whimsy nodded his shaggy head and trotted toward the driveway.

"Wait!" Jamie was running, not noticing his almost frozen feet. "Can I come see you sometime?" he asked, catching up.

"You can come if you want. I'll be with the herd. You may see me," said Whimsy.

Jamie began a slow, sad walk back to the house. The frozen ground hurt his feet.

15

Weeks passed. Jamie had called the rangers. They told him they had seen Whimsy with the herd. Jamie missed Whimsy. But he knew he had lost his pony for good.

Then one morning his dad announced, "Auction's tomorrow. Want to go?"

Jamie looked up from his pancakes. "I was going to ask *you* if we could go."

His dad smiled. "Then it's settled, although you'll have to skip school tomorrow."

Jamie grinned.

Friday morning Jamie and his dad hitched the horse trailer to the truck. They left right after breakfast.

The auction was much the same as the last time

except that it was too cold for there to be any flies. The horses weren't sweating this time. All the animals had fuzzy winter coats.

"I'll come with you to look them over before the sale begins," offered his dad.

"No thanks, Dad. My feet hurt a bit today. We can see them as they come into the ring."

Forty-nine horses and ponies were hustled into the ring, bid upon and sold. Forty-nine times Jamie shook his head, "No." Then came number 50. It was a three-year-old paint mare. White spots shone from her reddish brown body. Her coat was sleek. She was bigger than Whimsy. She had the long legs and deep chest of an animal that can run long distances.

"Let's start this beauty low at a hundred . . . hun'red . . . hun'red . . ." the auctioneer began his chant.

"One hundred!" Jamie yelled. His dad smiled.

The bid didn't go up very fast or as high as his dad thought it should on such a fine animal. "Perhaps there's something wrong with her that we haven't seen," he worried.

"Who'll gi' me two-fifty . . . fifty . . . fifty . . ."

"I'm sure she's fine, Dad," said Jamie. Then he yelled, "Two-fifty!" He looked at his father.

Jamie's dad nodded. He was thinking, She is a mare. At least she could have foals if for some reason she is no good to ride. And she is a beauty.

"Sold to the blond boy for two hundred and fifty dollars, and a real bargain she is!" called the auctioneer.

As the paint pony was led from the ring, Jamie was certain that she'd winked at him.